D1461604

Unillumined

by

Gary Beck

PURPLE UNICORN MEDIA

Published by Purple Unicorn Media

Unillumined
by Gary Beck

Author: Gary Beck
Contact via the publisher: info@purpleunicornmedia.com

Cover image by Robin Stacey

ISBN 978-1-915692-24-5

To the memory of Daemon Beck. Bright light,
too soon dimmed leaving us darker.

Poems from Unillumined have appeared in:

Dissident Voice, Epoque Press Ezine, Highland Park Poetry, Indian
Periodical, Kind of a Hurricane Press, Plum Tree Tavern, Polseguera
Magazine, The Orchards Poetry Journal
Verbal Arts (Authors Press), Vita Brevis Poetry Magazine (Vita
Brevis Press), Winamop Magazine

Table of Contents

Public Housing

I was born in the projects,
hot, sweaty in summer,
cold, shivering in winter.
I thought everyone lived like that
until I began to understand
what I saw on tv.
Some folks have a lot,
cars, mansions,
money to buy
anything they want.
I asked Momma's boyfriend,
Jamal, why some had everything
and we had nothing.
"You want what they got?"
"Yeah."
"How old you be?"
"Seven."
"You do things for me,
I give you money,
you get what you want."
"Enough to live somewhere else?"
"Thas up to you. Cool?"
"Yeah. Cool."

Art Revolution

The Industrial Revolution
created a timely fusion
between the emerging middle class
who no longer wanted
pictures of saints on their walls,
and the new artistes
recently freed from the shackles
that compelled subject matter,
allowing them to paint
landscapes, seascapes, still lifes,
as well as portraits
of the bourgeoisie,
perhaps flattering a little
the customers who paid
for art supplies,
non-artisan debauchery.

Inequality

Summer is over.
The last warming rays
disappear into the stratosphere
and may or may not come again.
Across America
struggling families
try to figure out
how to give their kids
a happy Halloween,
since they don't have money
for costumes, pumpkins, treats.
At the same time
super yacht season begins,
as billionaires rush to order
the latest amenities
they saw on their friend's yachts,
bigger swimming pool, spa,
submersible, helicopter,
whatever envy provides.
And as they wallow
in decadent opulence
on the sea going palace,
the homeless slowly submerge
into devouring streets,
unable to comprehend
a boat with golden faucets
as they scrounge for quarters.

Elegy On the Death of a Loved One

The pain of loss
so sharp
comfort and joy
depart
until I accept
the bright light
from her shining face
will be seen again
in memory only,
as long as I remember
the gift of knowing her.

Medical Visit

Another day at the hospital.
 A new department.
The clerk won't speak louder
so I can't hear her instructions.
She's impatient
when I ask questions.
Sheet after sheet of paper,
detailed instructions.
I don't have the concentration
to read all of it.
I hope I haven't signed away
still functioning body parts.
I hand the clerk the papers.
She's pleased to show me
what I didn't fill in,
where I didn't sign.
She takes my drivers license,
insurance cards, copies pictures.
Tells me the waiting period
is within an hour.
I ask, I thought reasonably,
'Why did I make an appointment
for a special time
if I have to wait that long?
She points me to the waiting area,
without a word.
Her cold eyes follow me
until I'm someone else's responsibility.
The waiting room is crowded.
Everyone looks unhappy.
Most are apprehensive.
I do not see a friendly face.
I do not think this place will help me,

but I must try,
in the hope of a little more life
before conclusion.

City Fixture

The homeless sit
on unrelenting streets
cardboard signs
advertising need.
Passersby seldom notice
the invisible men
hulking on concrete nests.

Learning Gap

The pace of life
changes incrementally,
the more we advance technically
the faster it moves.
In the middle ages
we knew how to make candles
and we had light,
dim perhaps,
but it banished darkness.
In the Information Age
we tell the A.I.
to put on the light,
without the faintest idea
how light works.
In another generation
we will be so advanced
that we ask A.I. for everything,
make nothing,
so when collapse occurs
we will be helpless
to prevent the fall.

Urban Nightmare

I walk decaying streets
of a crumbling city
submerging slowly
from the weight of wealth
crushing the superfluous
who do not serve the 1%.
Ghost shops everywhere
have signs 'for rent',
as small business people
can no longer afford
excessive rents, on-line competition
for goods and services.
In a caring society
there would be help
for the homeless,
the poverty population,
the struggling working class,
who do their duty
that sustains the system
with jobs, taxes, trade.
Instead, new buildings for the rich
devour fragile greenery,
until Mother Nature gasps for breath
future respiration in doubt.

Divided We Fall

The American Empire,
though we never called it that,
reached its peak
at the end of World War II
when we occupied
much of the world,
influenced the rest,
a military and industrial titan,
so strong, yet we needed an enemy
to keep the empire on a war footing,
to maintain sway as the dollar ruled.

Then the oligarchs decided
their interests didn't coincide
with the needs
of the American people.
They amassed more and more wealth,
spread it across the globe
and they were international.
They outsourced, downsized,
went offshore, hired robots,
anything for more profit.

And as the sinews of the nation,
the blue collar class
began to disappear,
we stopped making things
and bought from abroad,
which didn't benefit the people.

Then the melting pot cracked
and no one assimilated.
Divisiveness grew rampant

and our President
fueled the flames of dissension.
Compromise evaporated.

We stand on the precipice
of fatal collapse.
and are no longer sure
if we can heal our wounds,
survive endemic decay,
fostered by the uncaring rich.

Perverse Times

A child speaks to the world
about the threats of climate change.
President Trump mocks her.
The Treasury Secretary,
Trump's satellite,
a sterile bean counter,
insults her.
Other voices of ignorance
deride her.
She asks not for herself,
but for our only habitat
and its survival.
The madness we inflict
on our wounded environment
is further revealed
as so many scorn
the voice of a child,
crying in the wilderness.

Erratic Orbit

The sun rises late,
sets earlier,
but some of us hardly notice
bound to city cycles,
wake, rise, hygiene,
rush to work
on urban transit,
always late, crowded,
then the job
which many hate,
a survival necessity
like peasants of eld
tilling the fields
for bare sustenance,
then return home
on urban transit,
always late, crowded,
greet the family unit,
unsumptuous dinner,
park in front of the tv,
too tired for social media,
doze off, wake, hygiene,
then to sleep
to rise again,
no reward
only repetition
as the universe contracts
beyond our perception.

Gentrification

I live in an old tenement.
Friends and neighbors
I grew up with are gone.
They fixed up all the buildings
except mine,
which is why I still live here,
while all the other houses
is expensive
and the new people
who moved in
think they're special,
they look away when they see me.
They always stop and talk
and block the sidewalk
and won't move to let me by.
They all have funny looking dogs
and nanny ladies for their children.
Soon they'll fix my building.
I don't know where I'll go,
but I'll be glad
to get away from here.

The End of All Things

As the empire dissolves
madness accelerates,
breeding chaos.
Armed bands roam the country,
make dates
to fight other bands,
ignored by law enforcement.
The rich get richer
less and less concerned
with the well-being of others,
assuming the system
will continue to function
with fewer resources.
Opposing legislators
storm a congressional hearing,
similar to disorder past,
the Roman Senate,
the French Assembly,
and as dissolution looms
the great divide
between the haves
and the rest of us
grows wider,
while the deluded 1%
think they'll avoid disaster
whether in other countries,
or artificial enclaves
constructed in America
to provide comforts,
while the rest of us
go down in flames.

Suicide

Our negligent leaders
send young troops
to dangerous lands
where enemies abound
of all ages,
intent on death to America.
Our young soldiers
grow up with comforts
unknown to Afghanis,
where life of hardship
prepares them
for explosive vests,
detonating themselves
for God and masters,
while our stressed troops
are traumatized
from horrific conditions
that make them despair
of normal life
and kill themselves.

Causus Belli

Our soldiers volunteer
for military service
and most do not know
the foreign policies
that send them into danger.
They will fight, kill, die
for the good old USA
that is a different country
than the one they think they serve.
Most of them are young, inexperienced,
completely unaware
they are sent into combat
so the oligarchs can profit,
a bigger yacht
the exchange for Purple Hearts.

Fleeting Glimpse

I saw a monarch butterfly,
ephemeral beauty
in the concrete city,
flutter a moment
unnoticed by most,
no concept of time
so the brief life
feels complete.

Fading Sway

Once we had an empire
made it run,
worked on it all the time.
Built with guns and dollars
lots of fun,
as long as we had rule.
Once we had an empire
now its done,
leaving us without a dime.

Day of Reckoning

Avaricious Americans
stole almost half of Mexico.
We dismembered the Spanish Empire
and stole countries in the Pacific and Caribbean.
We undermined the British Empire,
let it bleed itself
of men and women
in World War I.
Then we destroyed
the German Empire,
the Japanese Empire,
the Soviet Empire,
and we inherited the earth.
We exercised authority
without responsibility,
exploiting, exhorting
friends and foes.
Now that our Empire
is dissolving,
the obese rich do not know
they'll be part of retribution.

Fantasia Number 1

All the Billionaires
should each give five million dollars
to set up a foundation
that will provide housing,
support services
to homeless families with children,
homeless veterans,
so those who served the nation,
innocent children
will be saved
from needless suffering.

Malnutrition

The leaves blow
across the dry land,
do not leave juice
to replenish the earth.
It doesn't matter in the city
where concrete abounds,
no wilderness,
only parks maintained
by part-time caretakers.

Callous Streets

Some walk the streets with purpose,
work, school, shopping,
all intent on accomplishment.
The homeless, mentally ill,
all the disadvantaged
who are not part of
the daily commitment
to meaningful activity
abandoned without trial
as they float to the surface
of the uncompassionate city
no longer concerned
with the dispossessed.

Call to Arms

The legions crossed land and sea
in service of the empire,
yet few of the troops
ever saw Rome,
an idea that birthed loyalty
in a time of barbarian lands,
or an unwanted occupation.
The legions did their duty
regardless of who ruled
and perhaps grew weaker
as corruption reigned,
hopefully not a model
for the good old USA,
with our many troops
far away.

Circumstantial Evidence

The days grow hotter.
The ice melts faster.
Nature is reeling
under relentless assault.
The owners of resources
that could halt the danger
to the only human habitat,
deny the claim of science
that global warming
is an increasing threat
to the continuation
of life on Earth.
Some of the wealthy
must have children,
yet they consume the future,
blind to our peril
that reveals the role model
 adopted by the lords of profit;
'Aprés moi, le déluge'.

Decomposing

As we age
the simple things
we once did effortlessly
now become a struggle,
incrementing frustration
until we deplete
remaining composure.

Trials

There are times that test us,
appraising our resolve
to endure disasters,
overcome poverty
in what always appears,
courtesy of the tv,
a prosperous world
arbitrarily denied
to many of us
without sound reason,
merit rarely easing
the daily struggle
to improve daunting conditions
that conspire to prevent
arrival to the comfort zone.

Institutionalization

I am confined to prison
in the cellblock of my mind,
sentenced without trial,
condemned to punishment
for high crimes,
greed, lust, envy,
the base appetites
that caused me to commit
unpardonable offenses.
My remaining hope
rehabilitation,
then parole
to start a new life,
hoping flames of temptation
weakness of will
may not trap me
back to recidivism.

Moving Along

At the turning point,
the course of time
erodes us
and we gradually lose
high vitality.
As decline speeds up
mental activity subsides
and we begin to resemble
the helpless infant,
without growth possibility.

Blind Taste

In the eighteenth century
the French aristos
consumed lavishly
every extravagance
in full view
of the impoverished people.
In the twenty first century
the aristos of wealth
consume lavishly,
but unlike earlier nobles
much of their wealth
not displayed publicly
for the impoverished people,
many still hopeful
for a bit of prosperity,
thus precluding
fervent revolution.

Precarious

We go from home to work,
school, shop, recreate
without recognizing
the terrible peril
that faces our land.
We have become urbanized,
easy to control,
totally dependent
on power, food supply, water,
easily discontinued
leaving us helpless,
existence improbable
except for small groups
outside the cities
now become death traps
for millions,
who cannot survive
without the necessities
that allow continuation.

Call to...

In the 1920s
after the disaster of World War I,
the German people were desperate
and while the wealthy
and well-to-do reveled,
the poor and needy seethed
with rage and frustration.
Fascist rallies
and extravagant promises
persuaded many to support
National Socialism
that vowed to revive Germany,
that led to
World War II,
the Holocaust.
If there are parallels today
with propaganda rallies,
pledges of imprisonment for some
and abuse of power
approved by many,
we can only hope
for a historical coincidence.

Blinded By Gold

The wealthy squander resources
in the pursuit of status,
building enormous mansions
striving to outdo their peers,
buying extravagant mega-yachts,
bigger, with more amenities
than their rivals,
so possessed by wanting
they have lost sight
of simple virtues.

Fantasia Number 2

Americans,
Republicans, Democrats
people of all beliefs,
despite differences
would unite in democracy,
rekindle the light
we once promised the world.

Seasonal Occurrences

The first day of Fall,
another seasonal change.
Yet the day feels like summer.
People walk the city streets
in short sleeve shirts,
most of us oblivious
to the threats of war,
Iran, China, Tau Ceti,
whoever can be used
to manipulate the people
that war always distracts
from the wrongdoing
of the owners of the country,
completely unconcerned
with the well-being
of the rest of us,
who go about our business
on a bright, sunny day
while we're being betrayed.

Revelations

When I was young
I was homeless
and learned the bitter lesson
of alienation, deprivation.
I remember winters
when my coat wasn't heavy enough
to keep out the cold.
But all the time in school
I heard noble words
that everyone believed,
but didn't apply to me.
Conditions changed for me
so I was never disadvantaged
in the land of the free
that I painfully discovered
was only for some of us.

Indistinct

When the elderly
reach a certain age
they begin to look alike,
walk alike,
talk alike,
become senile alike,
making some of us wonder
why there is so much hatred
for differences between us.

Judgements

The future society
will need doctors, nurses,
scientists, warriors to protect them,
certain workers
to get what they require
to keep things going
with the comforts they expect.
The internet and movies
are mandatory,
but liberal arts grads
are superfluous,
can only be afforded
if there's a surplus
of food, shelter, clothing.

Confinement

As concrete covers the land
greenery disappears
and we are manipulated
into urban clumps,
easily controlled
in an autocratic state.
Now that we're confined
in soaring hi-rises,
in congested cities
with only three day's supply
of food, pharmaceuticals,
rapidly depleted
when the power fails,
water cut off soon after,
leaving millions to perish
with no place for escape.

Devolved

Summer turns to Fall.
City people plod the streets,
heads down, backs bent,
already mourning
the last of warm days,
no longer connected
to the cycle of nature,
urbanized
beyond redemption.

Distress Call

Many Americans
struggling for survival
in a land of inequality,
still maintain
basic courtesy,
kindness, compassion
for others they know,
strangers passed for a moment,
none of them reflecting
the callous indifference
of prosperous leaders
insulated and removed
from daily exertion
to earn a livelihood
as the middle class economy
dissolves faster and faster,
eradicating security,
the promise of the Founding Fathers.

Too Cold

Winter winds blow early
chilling the land,
discomforting the people
who a few days ago
wore t-shirts
on a balmy Fall day.
Now huddling in down coats
they slouch on the streets
on the way to destinations,
unlike the abandoned homeless
shivering on concrete beds.

Do. Don't Talk

It is so easy
to criticize others,
complain endlessly
about abuses by government,
consume oneself in envy
of the extravagant rich,
instead of taking action
to improve this life,
contribute meaningfully
to a troubled society.

Wealth, the Religion of Ignorance

The super rich
do not know
millions of Americans
serve in the military,
build cars and planes
to take them to destinations,
all the skilled workers
who make the system
supposedly for the benefit of all,
but more often
only for the few,
devouring what should feed many,
yet each day
homeless children,
homeless veterans,
suffer deprivation
while the 1%
feast at tables of plenty.

21st Century Turmoil

The Presidency is under assault
one side from fear,
the other from greed.
We the people
have become suspicious
of everyone in Washington, D.C.,
justifiably.
They all take money
from their masters,
whine pitiably
when one has more than another.
In the past,
chaos was always part
of the American Way.
Now that we are in decline,
allies abandoned,
friends neglected,
enemies appeased,
some of us wonder
if we will be allowed
to dissolve into
a second world power,
or be torn apart
by inner dissension,
foreign attack.

Creature Comforts

The leaves are falling.
Autumn winds blow cooler.
We walk the streets a little faster
urged on by biting winds.
Yet throughout the land
there is no normalcy,
only seasonal change.
Most of us remain inside
in urban enclaves,
with advanced technology
that lets us stay at home
in inclement weather,
in a semblance
of a well-ordered life,
immune from climate,
except when disaster strikes,
catching us unprepared
for the struggle for survival.

Paean

I may not live to see
salvation of the earth
from ravages of climate change,
but I never give up hope
the well-meaning, the resourceful,
will recognize the dangers
before it's too late
and preserve a habitat
in the vast universe
for the aspirations
of a conflicted species
that still may rise
above its limitations.

Sterner Stuff

I never wanted
material prosperity.
Occasionally
I got sidetracked,
worked for money.
It didn't solve my inner anguish
that hungered for something purer
than unsatisfactory labor
for wages big or small
that didn't change my life,
consumed me in exertions
that didn't change the world,
burning aspirations
since early childhood
when I first encountered
American injustice.

Used Up

There are countless ills
in our troubled land
that once proclaimed
glorious ideals.
Now many live in poverty,
hope for a better future
diminishing daily,
while the servants of the rich
make endless promises
believed less and less
as hardship continues,
except for the wealthy,
so removed from compassion
they buy mega yachts,
while homeless children,
innocent of any crime,
are sentenced to despair,
homeless veterans
who saved the nation
indifferently discarded.

Unenlightened

I do not lament
the loss of youth,
loss of vitality,
but I cannot reconcile
my hope to improve the world
with the lack of accomplishment,
a bitter recognition
that still defies acceptance.

Conflict

An unexpected attack
kills a dangerous enemy
that provokes his nation,
always bitterly opposed
to hated America,
fervently wishing our destruction.
While at home
divided we stand,
the media and politicians
urge a circus
for personal gain
consistently demeaning
the country that nurtured them,
deluding the people
by asserting
free choice in a democracy.

Confused Country

After the President's rally,
I heard a lady say:
'I don't like what Trump says,
but I like what he does
for America'.
She didn't look prosperous
and she had two children
who weren't well-dressed,
so I had to wonder
if she knew what country she was in.
The Trump administration
is denying climate change,
destroying the environment,
abrogating treaties
with friends and allies,
piling up the national debt
so only the rich may prosper.
Did I really hear her say:
"America'.

Ignorance Is...

Americans walk the streets
oblivious to the threats
that face us daily
engineered by the oligarchs
who own our land,
who do not care
about the fate of the people
as long as they are served
by those who toil for the wealthy.
The rest of us
do not matter,
as long as we do not disturb
the pastimes of the rich.

Downturn

A Great Society
must have order,
not totalitarian control,
with a substantial infrastructure
so buses, subways, trains run,
planes fly, boats sail,
citizens go to work, school, play,
without being attacked,
illegally detained,
and everyone knows
tomorrow will function.
When doubt arises
that there will be continuation,
unease spreads like a plague.
Citizens turn to crime,
the system decays,
the environment erodes
and we accept the summons
to the third world.

High Crimes

Each day
the concept of democracy
erodes
faster and faster,
as servants of the rich
determine the future
of Americans
not wealthy or powerful enough
to control an election,
no longer given the illusion
that we have a say
in our way of life,
resources denied the people
in extravagant consuming
of a trillion dollars
to the rich and corporations.

Abuse of Office

People walk the streets
absorbed in their cares,
job, home, school,
while the servants of the oligarchs
legislate away
the environment,
the infrastructure,
blue collar jobs,
all in service of their masters
unconcerned with the needs
of the American people.

Vandals

What is beauty?
Many have asked.
But not often enough
to make the oblivious see
the wonders of the earth.
Can a Rothko, Rembrandt
compare to a glorious sunset?
Can Picasso, Matisse,
even Van Eyck
compare to a snow capped mountain?
Yet as a species
we have become dedicated
to the destruction of nature.

Tribulations

The great impeachment trial
may end today
with a foreordained verdict,
promised by the bought servants
of the oligarchs,
who decreed Trump innocent.
I believe he is unfit for office
and agree with the charges
against him,
only the surface of his crimes.
If there was a way
to insure he wouldn't be reelected
I would accept impeachment,
even though I didn't believe
it was best for the nation.
But I pity my country
if he is reelected
and continues to destroy
the fabric of America.

Too Soon

It is late February.
The trees are budding.
The birds are chirping:
'Spring. 'Spring'.
They do not know
Climate Change,
so when it freezes again
many will die
who prematurely molted
winter feathers.

Unstable Weather

It was warm yesterday.
The birds were happy,
chirping, feeding, arguing
about who took whose nest.
Today it's freezing.
The birds huddle together
not knowing
how winter came so quickly.
It won't do any good
for humans to explain
they are experiencing
Climate Change.

Urb State

The daily demands
to submit
in an urbanized land,
no one self-sufficient,
all dependent
on a non-familiar system,
most not knowing
where their food comes from,
millions doomed
when the water stops running.
The benefits of the city
a great convenience
in times of plenty,
a pitiless death trap
when the power fails.

Criteria

All of nature
dependent on
photosynthesis
upreaches urgently
for life giving rays
from the benevolent sun.
Only humans
ignore the need
for natural rejuvenation,
blinding ourselves
with confusing technology
that makes us forget
the urge to regenerate.

Score Board

Americans are not
a philosophic people
and tend to be pragmatic,
rather then contemplate
the nature of the universe,
which is why physicists
never get the attention
we give to sports stars.

Eternal Question

Each day terrible evils
soil the nation,
hurricanes, wars, crimes,
economic disasters,
yet most people go on,
live the rest of their lives,
overcoming adversity,
like our species has done
since we swung down
from the trees,
while those who suffer
do not understand
why others endure
and they do not.

Signs

After many false starts
it feels like spring today.
70 F. Clear skies. No wind.
People are sitting on the steps
of the Metropolitan Museum of Art.
Of course the mimes haven't come yet.
It's still too cold for them
to perform in front of the museum.
But people are happily walking
dogs, babies, the infirm,
despite the fears
of Coronavirus,
the other fears
that plague our country,
all is still calm.

Expedition

I have become
immersed in the city,
urban isolation
with only a glimpse
of renewing nature.
Then I take a bus
past Central Park,
an ordinary trip,
suddenly surprising
with lush greenery
that may not be
the forest primeval,
but wilderness enough
for me.

Park Interlude

Spring is near in Bryant Park.
Workman are disassembling
the skating rink structure
looming skeletally
over the foreign tourists
trying to figure out what it was.
The carousel waits for riders.
As the day warms
office workers rush for tables
for al fresco lunch.
By 1:00 p.m. the park is full.
Everyone but the homeless
enjoys a pleasant day,
thoughts of epidemic, recession,
briefly forgotten.

Idiocy Reigns

The weather changes rapidly
erratically, dynamically.
One Fall day it's 70F,
the next 95F,
the next 60F.
But our impaired leaders
do not believe in climate change
and our hapless president,
too busy tweeting, golfing,
asking for alligators
in the Rio Grande
to stop immigration,
will not do his duty
to protect and preserve
the future of the country.

Loyalties

The Kurds have been abandoned,
like other American allies
who served their purpose
supporting U.S. troops
on the battlefield,
suddenly superfluous
when policy changes
rendered indigenous services
unnecessary.
After gambling all
on pledges of support
against relentless foes
intent on extermination,
Kurds placed their hopes
on a powerful ally
who changed course,
left them behind,
no longer of consequence
in the world scheme of things.
It was like that in Vietnam,
when unable to defeat the North,
erosion of public support
prompted withdrawal,
abandoning vulnerable allies
who relied on us,
didn't survive out betrayal.

World Peace

New York City is never more crowded
than when the U.N. comes to town.
For one week,
courtesy of U.S. taxpayers,
delegates, heads of state
from all over the world
plot, scheme, party
at the expense of America,
who most hate,
despising us in the meeting halls,
using our restaurants, hotels, women,
while planning our destruction
under the auspices of
the world governing body.

A House Divided

America may be
in greater peril
than before
the Civil War.
Two opposing forces,
unreconcilable,
confront each other
verging on violence,
an ineffectual President,
worse than Buchanan,
will not stop the slide
to bitter conflict.
Difference between now and then
is most of us
huddle in cities,
vulnerable to disaster,
plague, flood, storm,
with no place to flee
the countryside, alien,
no longer welcoming
desperate refugees.
The only hope
a miraculous change
will transform the land
into a nation of harmony
and save us from ourselves.

Parade

Columbus Day Parade
New York City,
the biggest Italian-American
celebration in the world.
Hundreds of thousands
line the streets
most not really sure
what the Italian heritage is,
but it's a happy gathering,
the bands are playing,
the marchers are smiling,
a brief relief
from urban cares.

Threat Warnings

One day it's 95F,
the next it's 55F,
the ice keeps melting,
the seas get warmer,
the seas keep rising
devouring the shore.
The storms get bigger,
more destructive,
devastating a fragile land
where most people
live in cities,
so removed from nature
they cannot conceive
the speed of disaster
eroding vulnerable lives.

Suspicions of Mortality

The thighs of summer have departed
except for the brief flash
of a lush young body
exposing tantalizing flesh,
willing to pay the price
of chilled bones.
The beauties who displayed
for covetous eyes
are mostly covered now
and will not reveal
sleek skin until Spring,
and I do not know
if I will see them again.

Thanksgiving

The day before
the unique American holiday,
celebrating
how early settlers
in an untamed land
fooled the natives
into thinking they were friends.
It took a long time
for the locals to learn
that white man spoke
with forked tongue.
By then it was too late.
Most of them had been removed
to make room for immigrants.
Today there are so many
who don't have enough
to be thankful for,
perhaps the holiday
should be cancelled.

Some Do. Some Don't.

Those who have
are oblivious
on feast days,
stuffing themselves with good food,
watching the parade on tv,
watching the big game on tv,
while the dispossessed
do without,
times of plenty
an alien concept.

Time Lapse

The voices of winter
call in the new year,
hopeful on the eve,
eager to continue
positive concerns,
not yet resigned
to discontinuation.

Thwarted

Some of us strain
    each day
to do something better
    to improve
life for our children,
    our nation,
    the world.
Yet no matter how much
we exert ourselves
we rarely change
the nature of existence,
solutions elude us
since we lack power
to alter conditions.

Intolerance

America,
once beautiful
at least in myth,
our people struggling
to preserve the future,
despite exile from power.
The wealthy control
the means of subsistence
and may not allow
most of us to hope
for a better tomorrow.

Term of Office

Terrorism rises across the land.
A President faced with impeachment
orders military strikes
against Iranian extremists,
creating a crisis
as the Senate prepares
to dismiss all charges
against our patriotic leader
defending the nation
against all enemies,
domestic and foreign.

We Deceive

Despite the best efforts
of the well-meaning
deception undermines
the stability of nations,
different agendas,
needs, goals, ambitions
draw the greedy,
the power hungry
to always want more
at the expense of others,
making it impossible
for peace to prevail.

Warnings Ignored

An unusual warm day
in mid-January
doesn't fool the birds,
at least for the moment,
since they don't watch the news,
read government reports,
consequently
don't know about climate change
and are helpless victims
when global warming
brings cataclysmic change
consuming the environment
that allows life.

Vindication

Well, my fellow citizens,
after months of turmoil,
the impeachment of the President
draws to a close,
the circumstances preordained
by suborned senators,
serfs to the oligarchs
who would like Trump elected
for another four years
to continue to giveaway wealth
to corporations and the rich,
allow the fossil fuel industry
to continue to destroy
our fragile environment,
cut foodstamps for thousands,
divide the races, the nation,
and soon he'll be exonerated,
to crow in triumph
over his persecutors,
now vindicated,
and can blatantly proclaim
he is faultless,
the savior of America.

Confusion

The Tower of Babel
to some
a metaphor,
to others
a harsh reality
that we don't communicate,
or do it poorly,
or deceptively,
alienating many
because of dishonesty,
so good intentions
often crumble away
when we don't understand
opposing views.

A Plague on Both Their Houses

It is an election year
in the land of the free.
The democratic candidates
for the highest office
in the land of freedom
will have spent a billion dollars
by election time.
Meanwhile, our president,
a role model
for the greedy, the haters,
abuses the power of office,
abandons allies,
betrays friends,
pretends to know more than our Generals,
gives our money away
to corporations and the rich,
considered by many
the worst president ever,
yet the nation is so divided
he may be re-elected.

Deception

The trees began budding.
The sparrows bask in the sun
assuming it is spring.
People walk the tarnished streets
in light jackets, light sweaters,
some machos in t-shirts.
Then the temperature plummets.
Suddenly it's freezing.
Everyone bundles up
except the birds,
chirping piteously:
'we were the more deceived'.

Preference

If we are not taught
　　　　to look
when we are susceptible
　　　　children,
we may never learn
　　　　to see
the wonders of nature,
the wonders of man,
which makes us as a species
　　　　detached
from the beauties around us.
Of course some say
　　　　blindness
blots out the evils
that proliferate,
but better to lament
than wallow in ignorance.

Injustice For Many

So many vital issues,
with overload of information
from conflicting sources
so the average citizen
doesn't know what to believe.
Fortunately for the 1%
just as in every other lie,
the few determine for many.
And if they don't care
for the future of our planet
they will not act
to stop destruction,
so the good people
without power
are helpless to stop the fall.

We Request

I think the land
that gave me birth
the now endangered
Mother Earth
and only hope
we will not wait
to save the planet
before too late.

Printed in Great Britain
by Amazon

21331634R00058